ANNE HUTCHINSON

Fighter for Religious Freedom

Colonial Profiles Series

Dennis Brindell Fradin

Illustrations by Tom Dunnington
Picture Research: Judith B. Fradin

ENSLOW PUBLISHERS, INC.

Bloy St. & Ramsey Ave.
Box 777
Hillside, NJ 07205
U.S.A.

P.O. Box 38
Aldershot
Hants GU12 6BP
U.K.

Library of Congress Cataloging-in-Publication Data

Fradin, Dennis B.
Anne Hutchinson: fighter for religious freedom / by Dennis Brindell Fradin.
p. cm. — (Colonial profiles)
Includes index.
Summary: Recounts the story of the Puritan woman who was banished from her colony for being outspoken against the religious leaders there.
ISBN 0-89490-229-6
1. Hutchinson, Anne Marbury, 1591-1643—Juvenile literature.
2. Puritans—Massachusetts—Biography—Juvenile literature.
3. Massachusetts—History—Colonial period, ca. 1600-1775—Juvenile literature. [1. Hutchinson, Anne Marbury, 1591-1643.
2. Puritans.] I. Title. II. Series: Fradin, Dennis B. Colonial profiles.
F67.H92F73 1990
973.2'2'0924—dc 19
[B]
[92] 88-31329
CIP
AC

Printed in the United States of America

10 9 8 7 6 5 4 3 2 1

Illustration Credits:
Tom Dunnington (illustrator), pp. 9, 17, 18-19, 22, 28, 37, 39, 41; Courtesy of the Essex Institute, Salem, Massachusetts, p. 31; Historical Pictures Service, Chicago, pp. 10, 11, 12, 34, 43; Library of Congress, pp. 4, 14, 16, 24, 26.

Cover Illustration by Tom Dunnington.

Contents

Introduction 5

When She Was Anne Marbury.................. 7

"Well Beloved in England" 15

The Trip Across the Ocean 21

"She Did Much Good in Our Town" 23

Powerful Enemies.. 27

Anne's Two Trials... 33

Anne Hutchinson in Rhode Island and New York... 38

Important Dates.. 44

Glossary 45

Index 47

A statue of Anne Hutchinson and one of her children

Introduction

Today Americans can worship as they please. They can change religions. They can make up new ones. If they want, they can have no religion. This is called freedom of worship. The United States began to protect this basic right in 1791. That was just a few years after the birth of the United States in 1776.

Before the United States was born, England ruled the 13 American colonies from 1607 to 1776. During those years, many Europeans came to America in search of religious freedom. The colonies did not offer religious freedom to all, though. People of certain faiths could not live in many places. Those who argued with religious leaders were jailed or forced to move. Some were even hanged.

A number of colonial Americans risked their lives to fight for religious freedom. Anne Hutchinson was one of the first. Anne was the mother of a large family that came from England to Massachusetts in 1634. Anne lost her battle. But she helped pave the way for later Americans to make freedom of religion the law of the land.

When She Was Anne Marbury

Anne Marbury was born in July 1591 in Alford, a small town in eastern England. Her father, Francis Marbury, was a minister and teacher. He worked for the Church of England—the country's official religion. But Reverend Marbury did something risky. He criticized the Church of England. He said ministers should have more schooling. He said there should be more of them, so small towns could have their own ministers.

Reverend Marbury's words reached government officials. He was punished for speaking against the church. By age 23 he had been jailed three times for doing so. About the time of Anne's birth, Francis Marbury spoke out again. This time he avoided jail. But he was taken off his job as teacher and preacher. He could not go back to work until 1594, when Anne was three years old.

Little is known of Anne's early years. In her

time, few girls had much schooling. There is no record that Anne ever went to school. Her father probably taught her at home, however. The two of them probably read and discussed the Bible. Perhaps he taught her to question the beliefs of the time.

Had she been a boy, Anne would have gone to college. Three of her brothers earned college degrees. Back then, though, girls could not go to college. Instead, Anne stayed home and helped her mother care for the family.

And what a large family it was! Anne was the third of 14 children born to Francis and Bridget Marbury. Anne also had two half-sisters born to her father's first wife, who had died young. As an adult, Anne was a skilled nurse and midwife (a person who helps women give birth). She probably learned nursing by caring for her sisters and brothers. She may have learned to be a midwife by helping her own mother deliver babies.

As he grew older, Francis Marbury spoke out less. With all those children, he could not afford to lose his job or be jailed again. During the early 1600s, however, many other people opposed the Church of England.

Some left the Church of England and formed their own churches. These people were called Separatists. The Separatists held services in barns and homes. But English officials learned of these

Anne as a child studying with her father

People in England sometimes had to sit in the stocks as punishment. The stocks held their legs.

meetings. They fired many Separatists from their jobs. They threw some of them in jail.

A larger group stayed within the Church of England while trying to improve it. These people were called Puritans. They wanted to focus more on the Bible. They wanted simpler church services.

The Puritans were picked on, too. In 1605 about 300 Puritan ministers lost their jobs. Suddenly there was a shortage of ministers. Anne's father applied for a job in London. In 1605 he was named minister at St. Martin in the Vintry Church in London.

These English people are secretly holding a prayer meeting in a home because they do not want officials to know about it.

London, England, in the 1600s

It took about 10 days for the Hutchinsons to make the 140-mile trip to their new home in London. England's capital must have amazed 14-year-old Anne. Alford had just several hundred people, most of whom she knew. London had a quarter of a million people. In some places London had more people in one block than lived in all of Alford. London was also England's center for the arts. The famous playwright William Shakespeare was one of the creative people working in London.

The Marburys had been in London two years when great news reached England from America. In spring of 1607 Englishmen had built a town in Virginia and named it for King James I. Jamestown was England's first permanent American town.

America was huge. England's Separatists and Puritans thought of a way to escape persecution. They could build their own colonies in America. Anne heard such talk. She could not have known that her future was in the New World, too.

St. Botolph's Church in Boston, England

"Well Beloved in England"

Anne's father died in early 1611. Anne grieved for him. She was upset for another reason. In those days, English women did not go out to live alone. They stayed at home until they married. Anne wanted a family of her own, but she had no marriage prospects. Francis Marbury's death made it look as though Anne would spend her life caring for her brothers and sisters.

Then, near Anne's 21st birthday, a young man from her hometown of Alford called at her London home. He was William Hutchinson, a merchant and sheep farmer. The two young people liked each other very much. In August 1612 they were married.

William and Anne Hutchinson moved back to Alford to live. Soon after the move, Anne learned that Reverend John Cotton had been hired by St. Botolph's Church in Boston, England. Cotton was a brilliant preacher. Anne and William decided to make the 25-mile trip from Alford to Boston to hear him. They went on horseback.

Anne loved John Cotton's preaching. He believed in Puritan ideas. He tried to simplify services. He wanted to focus more on the Bible. Compared to other ministers, he saw God as kind instead of cruel.

Soon Anne and William were going to St. Botolph's often. But it was not enough for Anne just to hear Reverend Cotton. She wanted to talk about his ideas with other people. Anne began

Reverend John Cotton

Anne and William Hutchinson riding horseback to Boston, England

holding meetings in her home for the women in the area. At these meetings, she led talks on Reverend Cotton's sermons and other religious subjects.

Anne and William also raised a large family during their 22 years in Alford. Their first child, Edward, was born in 1613. Then came Susanna, Richard, Faith, Bridget, Francis, Elizabeth, William, Samuel, Anne, Mary, and Katherine. Susanna, William, and Elizabeth died young. It was a custom to give new children the names of

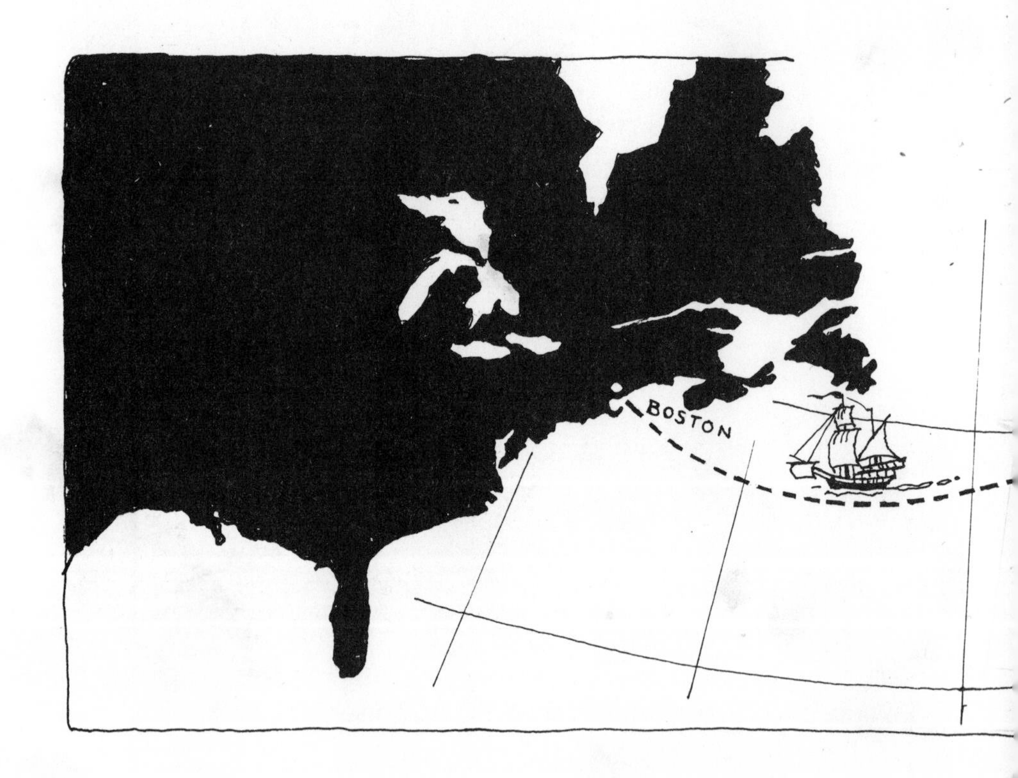

ones who had died. When the Hutchinsons' 13th child was born in 1631, they named him William. When their 14th was born in 1633, they named her Susanna.

Besides raising her own family, Anne Hutchinson was "well beloved in England at Alford," as John Cotton later wrote. She was a fine midwife and nurse whose friendly, gentle ways soothed people. As the years passed, more and more women came to Anne's meetings.

For many years John Cotton preached in

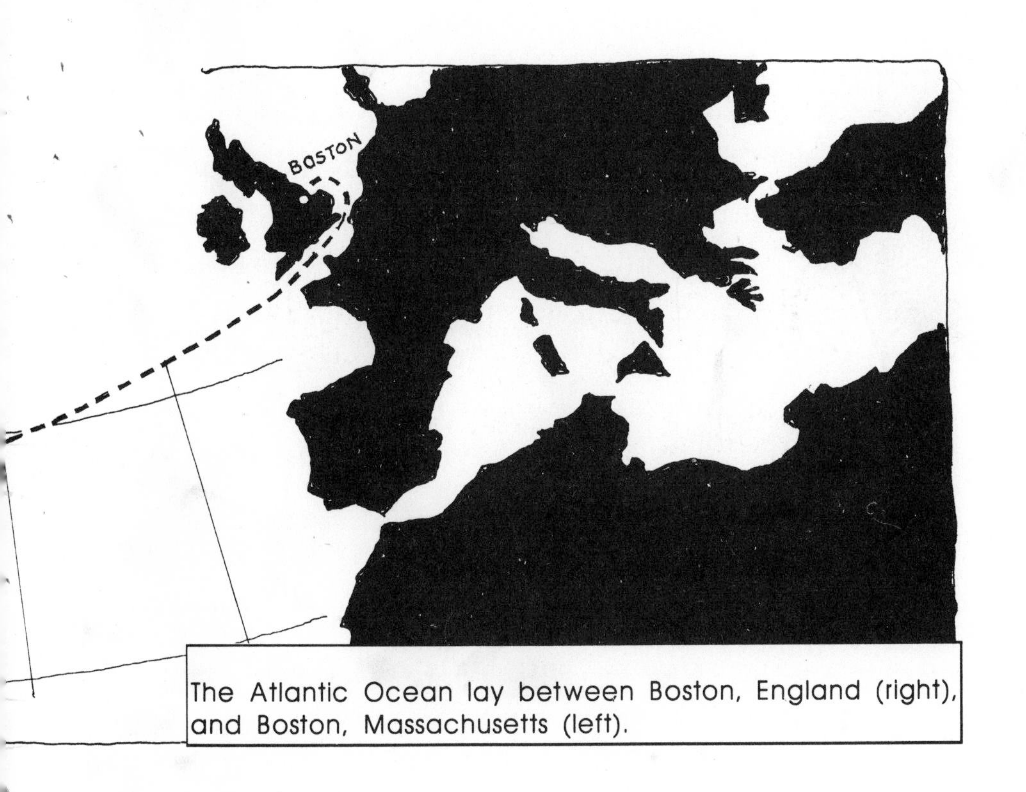

The Atlantic Ocean lay between Boston, England (right), and Boston, Massachusetts (left).

peace. It was said that King James I liked Cotton and protected him. But under the next king, Charles I, Reverend Cotton's ideas brought him trouble. When he learned that officials were looking for him, Cotton fled to London. In summer 1633 he sailed to America.

By that time, there were two English colonies in what is now Massachusetts. A group of English Separatists known as Pilgrims had started the Plymouth Colony in 1620. About 10 years later, Puritans had founded the Massachusetts Bay Colony, with Boston as its hub. Reverend Cotton went to Boston, Massachusetts. The Puritans had named the town for Boston, England.

The Hutchinsons had hoped to sail with Reverend Cotton to Massachusetts. They would have gone to the ends of the earth to hear him preach. But Anne was pregnant with the second Susanna. She could not make the ocean crossing. Two Hutchinsons did go with Reverend Cotton. One was 20-year-old Edward, their oldest child. The other was William's youngest brother, also named Edward.

Susanna's birth went smoothly late in 1633. Anne and William then packed for the long trip to America.

The Trip Across the Ocean

In spring 1634 the Hutchinsons left their home in Alford. They went to London, from where their ship would sail. In late July 1634 Anne, William, and the 10 children boarded the *Griffin*. The ship soon set sail.

In those days, it took several months to cross the Atlantic Ocean. The people on the *Griffin* passed the time by listening to Zechariah Symmes preach. Symmes, a Puritan minister, often spoke for five hours straight. He spoke of a harsh God who could only be won over if people did good deeds. Anne believed in a more loving God. Not only that, but Reverend Symmes looked down on women.

Finally, Anne exploded. She yelled at Reverend Symmes. In those days, women were supposed to obey their husbands and ministers. It was rare for a woman to yell at a minister. Anne walked out of the large cabin where

Reverend Symmes was preaching. As she did so, Symmes said he would cause her trouble once they reached Boston.

Anne yelling at Reverend Symmes on shipboard

"She Did Much Good in Our Town"

The *Griffin* reached Boston in September 1634, after a two-month voyage. Only the Puritan religion was allowed in Massachusetts Bay. Anne and William asked to join Boston's Puritan Church. John Wilson and John Cotton were its ministers. William Hutchinson was admitted several weeks later. Partly due to Reverend Symmes, Anne had to wait a few extra days. Other than that, for several years things went well for Anne.

The Hutchinsons obtained land on the corner of Boston's High Street and Sentry Lane. Workmen built them a two-story frame house. Across the street lived John Winthrop, the Massachusetts Bay Colony's main founder. John Cotton and his wife also lived nearby.

Anne soon became very popular. As John Cotton later wrote, she "did much good in our town" as a midwife and nurse. She also held religious

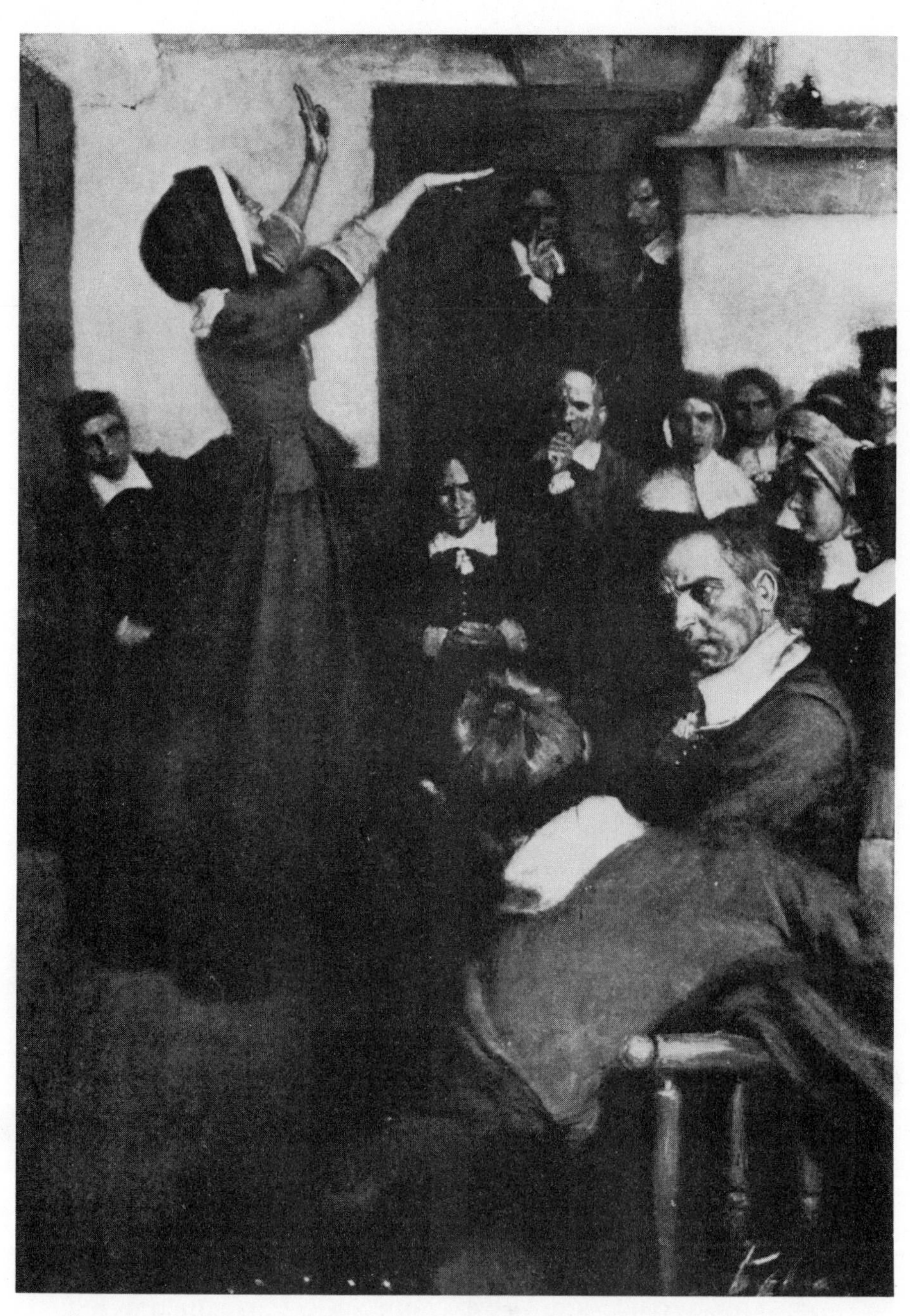

Anne Hutchinson preaching in her home in Boston, Massachusetts

meetings, as she had done in England. At first just 6 or 7 women met with Anne in her home. But the number grew to 20, then 50. Anne sat in a big chair leading the talks about John Cotton's sermons and other matters.

Women told their husbands about Anne's ideas of a loving God. Men began coming to her meetings, too. Soon so many people were coming that Anne had to host two weekly meetings. The Monday one was for men and women. The Thursday meeting was just for women. Up to 80 people at a time came. Among them were some leading Bostonians.

Everything seemed to be going Anne's way. In March 1636 she gave birth to her 15th and last child. Anne and William named him Zuriel. Two months later one of Anne's friends, 23-year-old Henry Vane, was elected Massachusetts governor. The day after that, Anne's brother-in-law John Wheelwright arrived from England. A minister from a town near Alford, John Wheelwright shared many of Anne's views.

Governor Vane treated Anne like a great religious leader. Even Boston's children went around asking each other if their parents believed in Anne's ideas. As her fame spread, people from other Massachusetts towns like Salem and Roxbury came to her meetings.

With all this support, Anne grew bolder. She told people they did not need ministers to teach them God's ways. They could know God on their own. She told people to pray only when they felt like it. She criticized Reverend Wilson and some other Massachusetts ministers. She said that John Cotton and John Wheelwright were the colony's only two good ministers. Anne even led some people out of church during Reverend Wilson's sermons. She made enemies by doing these things.

Henry Vane

Powerful Enemies

Through his window across the way, John Winthrop watched people crowd into Anne's house. Winthrop, who was nearly 50 years old, was angry and jealous. A few years earlier, in 1630, he had led the founding of Boston. He had been Massachusetts' first governor. He had hoped to be governor all his life. But in 1636 Winthrop had been voted out of office. He had been beaten by Henry Vane, an Anne Hutchinson supporter who was young enough to be his son.

John Wilson also disliked Anne. His dislike grew stronger when Anne tried to remove him as minister of the Boston church. She wanted John Wheelwright to replace him. This might have happened, but John Cotton helped save Wilson's job. Cotton had his own rivalry with Reverend Wilson. He thought Anne was becoming too powerful, though. He also opposed her on some points. Cotton thought people needed ministers.

John Winthrop watching jealously through his window as people come to hear Anne preach

He did not think that people should pray just when the mood struck.

By late 1636 a struggle for control of Massachusetts had begun. Governor Vane and Anne Hutchinson led one side. They wanted less-strict government and religion. They thought people had the right to speak and act as they wished, if no one was harmed. The other side was led by John Winthrop and John Wilson. They thought that God was harsh and that government should be, too. They thought people should not be allowed to argue with authorities.

Most Bostonians sided with Anne Hutchinson and Governor Vane. But in Massachusetts' country towns, many people supported Winthrop and Wilson. John Cotton was caught in the middle. He agreed with many of Anne's ideas. Yet he was afraid to oppose John Winthrop and Reverend Wilson.

John Winthrop was a lawyer. He began using Massachusetts' laws to get his way. Most Bostonians wanted John Wheelwright to be added to the staff of the church. Winthrop found a way to block him. There was a little-known rule that *every* church member had to approve a new minister. Winthrop stood up alone. He objected to Anne's brother-in-law. Wheelwright had to take a job as minister 10 miles from Boston.

Winthrop also found a way to become governor again. He helped arrange to hold the 1637 election west of Boston at Cambridge, Massachusetts. Winthrop had many more friends than Vane around Cambridge. Besides, many Vane supporters could not get to Cambridge. As a result, John Winthrop was elected Massachusetts governor in May 1637. Henry Vane was defeated and returned to England.

Governor Winthrop struck at his foes. He helped pass a law to keep certain people out of Massachusetts. The purpose was to keep out Anne Hutchinson supporters.

Religion and law were mixed together in Massachusetts. Anyone who broke Puritan rules also broke Massachusetts law. For example, those who missed church or swore could be whipped or locked in the pillory. A month before he became governor, Winthrop and his friends had placed John Wheelwright on trial. Reverend Wheelwright had given a sermon supporting Anne Hutchinson's ideas. The Massachusetts court had found Wheelwright guilty of trying to harm the colony. But Wheelwright's sentence had been put off until after the election.

In November 1637 Governor Winthrop gave Wheelwright a harsh sentence. He banished him from the colony. This meant he had to go into

Reverend John Wheelwright

the wilderness to find a new home. Indians and wild animals made this dangerous. Anne and William Hutchinson said good-bye to their brother-in-law. Wheelwright left Massachusetts and went north to New Hampshire. In 1638 he founded the town of Exeter there.

Soon after Wheelwright was banished, Anne Hutchinson was placed on trial. She knew her only chance was to promise to change her ways. But on a cold November day in 1637 Anne entered the courtroom with her head high and a fierce look in her eyes.

Anne's Two Trials

Anne was angry, and for good reason. At her trial, Anne could not have any witnesses on her side. All the witnesses would be against her. John Winthrop broke the law by doing something even more unfair. He was not only the chief lawyer against her. He was also the chief judge. Imagine being tried by a judge who hated you!

"What have I said or done?" Anne snapped at Winthrop, as the trial began.

Anne had criticized the ministers, Winthrop said. She had also taught religion to men at her meetings. Men should teach women, Winthrop claimed—not the other way around. Winthrop brought witness after witness against her. Deputy Governor Thomas Dudley said Anne had caused all the colony's problems. Reverend Symmes told of his shipboard fight with Anne.

Only several people took Anne's side. John Cotton spoke up for her. William Coddington, a

Anne's first trial

man at the trial, complained that Winthrop was judge. "No man may be a judge and an accuser, too," he said. Winthrop told Coddington to be quiet. A few minutes later Winthrop and the other judges ordered Anne banished.

"I desire to know wherefore [why] I am banished?" Anne angrily said.

But Winthrop would not tell her why. "Say no more, the court knows wherefore and is satisfied," he said. This ended her trial. Some of Anne's friends were also ordered to leave Massachusetts.

Winter was coming. Not even Anne's enemies wanted her to make a winter trip through the wilderness. Anne was allowed to stay in Massachusetts until spring, but she was imprisoned in a home. William Hutchinson left the older children in charge of the younger ones. Then he went out to find a new home. He, William Coddington, and several other Massachusetts people bought land from the Indians in Rhode Island. They began building a settlement there.

In March 1638 Anne was given a second trial. This one was to decide if she should be thrown out of the Puritan Church. Anne's judges this time were Reverend Wilson and other church officials. Compared to her treatment at this trial, John Winthrop had been gentle.

Anne was pregnant and feeling ill at the time. But the ministers hammered away at her hour after hour in the church. Reverend Wilson called her an "instrument of the Devil." Reverend Thomas Shepard called her "a very dangerous woman." John Cotton agreed with Anne on many points. But now he turned on her to show that he sided with his fellow ministers. He told Anne that "the poison" of her ideas outweighed the good she had done.

At the end of this trial, Reverend Wilson threw Anne out of the Puritan Church. "I do deliver you up to Satan [the Devil]," said Wilson. Anne's friend Mary Dyer rose and walked with her out of the church.

Anne Hutchinson and Mary Dyer walking out of the church together

Anne Hutchinson in Rhode Island and New York

A few days after her second trial, Anne left Massachusetts. She and her children traveled 65 miles from Boston to their new home in Rhode Island. After traveling on foot and by canoe for a week, they met William on Aquidneck Island. Anne helped found the town of Portsmouth there. It was Rhode Island's second English town.

Not long after coming to Rhode Island, Anne had a miscarriage. She may have lost her unborn baby partly because of her troubles and the hard trip. But when Massachusetts officials learned of this, they said God had punished Anne for being evil.

The Rhode Island Colony had been founded in 1636 by Roger Williams. Like Anne Hutchinson, Williams had been driven from Massachusetts for his religious beliefs. Also like Anne, Williams thought people had the right to worship as they

Anne and William reunited in Rhode Island. He has already built a house for them.

pleased. He had set up such a system in Rhode Island.

Massachusetts people looked down on Rhode Island for giving people so much freedom. They called it "Rogue Island." From time to time Massachusetts officials came to Rhode Island. They visited people who had left Massachusetts. Those who said they had changed their ways might be allowed back into Massachusetts.

Three Massachusetts men paid such a visit to Anne and William Hutchinson. They told Anne they were from the church of Boston. They waited to see if she would beg for mercy. Anne angrily told them, "I know no such church." Next they tried to get William to condemn Anne's ideas. William refused. "I am more tied to my wife than to the church," he said. "I look upon her as a dear saint and servant of God."

In 1642 William Hutchinson died. There was talk that Rhode Island would soon become part of Massachusetts. Anne feared that, if this happened, Massachusetts officials would come after her. She decided to go to New York with her children who were still at home. They moved to a remote place not far from present-day New York City.

In 1643 the New York governor ordered many peaceful Indians in the area killed. When things like this happened, the Indians sometimes struck

Anne and William telling off three visitors from Massachusetts

back at farm families. In late summer 1643 the Indians killed a number of colonists. Among them were Anne Hutchinson and five of her children.

Back in Rhode Island, Massachusetts, and England, many people mourned her. But John Winthrop wrote that with Anne dead and her friends banished, no one was left in Massachusetts "to disturb our sweet peace." Much of what we know about Anne Hutchinson comes from Winthrop's writings. He wanted to warn people about ideas like hers. Instead, thanks partly to Winthrop's writings, Anne Hutchinson is hailed as one of America's first fighters for religious freedom.

The murder of Anne Hutchinson and five of her children

Important Dates

1591 Anne Marbury is born in Alford, England.

1605 Anne and her family move to London.

1611 Francis Marbury, Anne's father, dies.

1612 Anne marries William Hutchinson; also this year Reverend John Cotton goes to work at St. Botolph's Church in Boston, England.

1613 Edward, first of their children, is born to Anne and William Hutchinson.

1633 Reverend John Cotton sails to Boston, Massachusetts.

1634 The Hutchinsons sail to Boston, Massachusetts.

1636 Zuriel, last of their 15 children, is born to Anne and William; also this year Anne's friend Henry Vane is elected governor of Massachusetts.

1637 John Winthrop unseats Vane as governor; Anne's first trial is held late in the year, and she is ordered banished.

1638 Anne is thrown out of the Puritan Church and out of Massachusetts; she joins William in Rhode Island.

1642 William Hutchinson dies.

1643 Anne Hutchinson and five of her children are killed by Indians in what is now New York State.

Glossary

authorities—people in charge.

banished—forced to leave a place.

colony—a settlement built by a country outside its borders.

criticize—to find fault with.

freedom of worship—the freedom to express one's religious beliefs the way one wants.

governor—the leader of a colony or state.

mercy—kindness and forgiveness.

midwife—a person who helps women give birth.

miscarriage—the natural death of an unborn baby.

New World—a nickname for the Americas.

Pilgrims—the people who built Plymouth, England's first settlement in Massachusetts.

pillory—a device for punishment that held a person's arms and head.

pregnant—expecting a baby.

Puritans—people who stayed inside the Church of England but tried to improve it.

religion—a set of beliefs concerning God or gods.

rivalry—competition between two or more people.

saint—a very holy person.

Separatists—people who left the Church of England.

sermon—a religious talk.

INDEX

Alford, England, 7, 13, 15, 18, 19, 25
Atlantic Ocean, *18-19*, 21

Boston, England, *14*, 15, *18-19*, 20
Boston, Massachusetts, *18-19*, 20, 22, 23, 25, 27, 29, 30, 38

Cambridge, Massachusetts, 30
Church of England, 7, 8, 11. *See also* Puritans.
Coddington, William, 33, 35
Cotton, Reverend John, 15, *16*, 18, 19, 23, 25, 26, 27, 29, 33, 36
  preaching of, 16, 19-20
  sails to America, 20

Dudley, Thomas, 33
Dyer, Mary, 36, *37*

England's rule over the 13 colonies, 5
Exeter, New Hampshire, founding of, 32

Griffin, 21, 23

Hutchinson, Anne, 5
  appearance of, *4*
  banishment of, 35, 38, *39*
  birth of, 7
  childhood of, 7-8, *9*
  children of, *4, 18-19, 20, 21, 25, 35, 38, 42, 43*
  death of, 42, *43*
  education of, 8, *9*
  enemies of, 26, 27-32
  founding Portsmouth, Rhode Island Colony, 38
  London home, 13, 15
  marries William Hutchinson, 15
  as midwife/nurse, 8, 19, 23
  New York home, 40
  preaching by, 18, 19, *24*, 25, 26
  Rhode Island home, 38, *39*
  sails to America, 21-*22*
  trials of, 32, 33-36
Hutchinson, William, 15, 16, *17*, 18, 20, 21, 23, 25, 38
  building Rhode Island home, 35
  death of, 40
  defending Anne's ideas, 40, *41*

Indians, 32, 40, 42, *43*

Jamestown, Virginia, 13

King Charles I, 20
King James I, 13, 20

London, England, *12*, 13, 21

Marbury, Reverend Francis, 7, 8, *9*
    death of, 15
    punishment of, 7
    at St. Martin in the Vintry Church in London, 11

Massachusetts, 5, 20, 35, 38, 40, 42
    fight for control of, 29
    laws of, 30
Massachusetts Bay Colony, 20, 23

Pilgrims, 20
Plymouth Colony, 20
punishment methods, 5, *10*, 11, 30
Puritan Church, Boston, 23, 27, 29, 36, *37*, 40
Puritans, 11, 13, 20, 23

religion
    freedom of, 5, 42
    persecution because of, 5, 13, 30
Rhode Island Colony, 35, 38, 40, 42

Separatists, 8, 11, 13, 20
Shakespeare, William, 13
Shepard, Reverend Thomas, 36
St. Botolph's Church, *14*, 15
stocks. *See* punishment methods.
Symmes, Reverend Zechariah, 21, *22*, 23, 33

Vane, Henry, 25, *26*, 27, 29, 30
Virginia, 13

Wheelwright, Reverend John, 25, 26, 27, 29, 30, *31*, 32
Williams, Roger, 38
Wilson, Reverend John, 23, 26, 27, 29, 35, 36
Winthrop, John, 23, 27, *28*, 29, 30, 32, 33, 35, 42
worship, freedom of, 5